CW01666745

THAI *Cuisine*

Berryland Books

0 9 8 7 6 5 4 3

Managing Editor: Richard Johnston
Author: Dr. Anita Shan
Designer: Prof. Madhu Krishna, Signet Designs, India.

Printed and bound in China
ISBN 1-84577-622

A catalogue record of this book is available from the British Library

NB: Recipes using uncooked eggs or meat or fish should be avoided by infants, the elderly, pregnant women and anyone suffering from an illness.

Contents

Appetizers
Spring rolls 04
Corn fritters 06
Pork satay with sauce 08

Soups & Salads
Vegetable soup with strips of omelette 10
Chicken and coconut soup 12
Hot and sour prawn soup 14
Thai vegetable soup 16
Glass noodle salad with shrimp 18
Spicy seafood salad 20

Main course
Green chicken curry 22
Vegetable Thai curry 24
Steamed fish with chilly sauce 26
Beef in peanut sauce 28
Stir-Fried vegetables with sesame and rice 30
Beef fried rice 32
Spicy fried noodles with meat 34
Thai fried noodles with tofu and shrimps 36
Sweet and hot noodles with vegetables & chicken 38
Chicken curry with Thai basil, peppers and rice 40

Desserts
Banana fritters 42
Sticky rice with mango wedges 44

Conversion Guide 46
Glossary 48

Spring rolls

Makes 25

Ingredients

- 9½ X 6in (24 X 15cm) square spring roll wrappers
- 2tbsp (30ml) plain all purpose flour
- Vegetable oil for deep frying
- Chilli sauce to serve

For the filling

- 4-6 Chinese dried mushrooms, soaked for 30 minutes in warm water to cover
- 2oz (60g) cellophane noodles
- 2 garlic cloves, finely chopped
- 3 fresh red chillies, seeded and chopped
- 8oz (250g) minced pork or chicken
- 2oz (60g) peeled prawns
- 2tbsp (30ml) Thai fish sauce
- 1tsp (5ml) granulated sugar
- 1 carrot, grated
- 2oz (60g) canned bamboo shoot, drained and chopped
- 2oz (60g) bean sprouts
- 2 spring onions (scallions), finely chopped
- 1tbsp (15ml) chopped cilantro (coriander)
- ¼tsp (1ml) freshly ground pepper
- 2tbsp (30ml) oil for frying

Method

1 Drain and chop the mushrooms.

2 Place the noodles in a large bowl, pour boiling water until covered and soak for 10minutes or until soft. Drain and snip them into 2in (5cm) lengths.

3 Heat oil in a wok, add the garlic and chillies and stir-fry for 30sec. Set aside. Add the chicken or pork to the wok and stir-fry until cooked.

4 Add the mushrooms, noodles and prawns. Stir in the fish sauce and sugar and add the pepper.

5 Tip the mixture into a bowl. Stir in the grated carrot, chopped bamboo shoot, bean sprouts, spring onions and chopped coriander. Add the chilli, garlic mixture and mix well.

6 Unwrap the spring roll wrappers. Put the flour in a small bowl and stir in a little water to make a paste. Place a spoonful of the filling in the centre of the spring roll wrapper.

7 Turn the bottom edge over to cover the filling, then fold the sides. Roll up the wrapper almost to the top and brush the edges with the flour paste and seal.

8 Heat the oil and fry the spring rolls until crisp and golden. Drain on kitchen paper and serve hot with chilli sauce.

Corn fritters

Makes 12

Ingredients

- Kernels of 3 corn cobs weighing 8oz (250g)
- 1 garlic clove, crushed
- Small bunch of fresh cilantro (coriander), chopped
- 2 green chillies finely chopped
- 1 scallion (spring onion) finely chopped
- 1tbsp (15ml) soy sauce
- 3oz (90g) rice flour or all-purpose (plain) flour
- 2 eggs, lightly beaten
- 2fl oz (60ml) cup water
- Salt and freshly ground black pepper
- Oil for frying
- Sweet chilli sauce to serve

Method

1 Place the kernels in a bowl. Add garlic, coriander, green chilli, spring onion, soy sauce, flour, eggs and water and mix well.

2 Season the above with salt and pepper to taste and mix again. The mixture should be firm enough to shape, but not stiff.

3 Heat oil, add spoonfuls of the corn mixture and fry until golden brown.

4 Drain on kitchen paper and serve hot with chilli sauce.

Pork satay with sauce

Makes 20

Ingredients

- 16oz (500g) lean pork
- 1tsp (5ml) grated root ginger
- 1 stalk lemon grass, finely chopped
- 3 garlic cloves, finely chopped
- 1tbsp (15ml) medium curry paste
- 1tsp (5ml) ground cumin
- 1tsp (5ml) ground turmeric
- 4tbsp (60ml) coconut cream
- 2tbsp (30ml) fish sauce
- 1tsp (5ml) granulated sugar
- 20 wooden skewers
- Oil for cooking

For the sauce

- 8fl oz (250ml) coconut milk
- 2tbsp (30ml) red curry paste
- 3oz (90g) crunchy peanut butter
- 4fl oz (125ml) chicken stock
- 3tbsp (45ml) brown sugar
- 2tbsp (30ml) tamarind juice
- 1tbsp (15ml) fish sauce
- Salt as desired

Method

1 Cut the pork into 2in (5cm) strips. Mix together ginger, lemon grass, garlic, curry paste, cumin, turmeric, coconut cream, fish sauce and sugar.

2 Pour over pork and marinate for 2 hours.

3 Prepare the sauce. Heat the coconut milk over low heat. Add the red curry paste, peanut butter, chicken stock and brown sugar.

4 Stir for 5-6 minutes. Add the tamarind juice, fish sauce and salt to taste.

5 Thread the meat on the skewers. Brush with oil and grill for 3-4 minutes on each side until cooked. Serve with satay sauce.

Vegetable soup with strips of omelette

Serves 4

Ingredients

- 1 egg
- 1tbsp (15ml) peanut oil
- 30fl oz (900ml) vegetable stock
- 2 large carrots, finely diced
- 2 outer leaves savoy or Chinese cabbage, shredded
- A few cauliflower florets, cleaned
- 2tbsp (30ml) soy sauce
- ½tsp (2½ml) granulated sugar
- ½tsp (2½ml) ground black pepper
- Fresh cilantro (coriander) to garnish

Method

1 Heat oil in a pan. Pour the beaten egg and swirl the pan to coat the base evenly. Cook over medium heat and slide the omelette out of the pan. Roll the omelette and slice into ¼in (6mm) rounds. Set aside for garnish.

2 Pour the stock into a large pan. Bring to a boil the carrots, cabbage and cauliflower florets. Reduce heat and add soy sauce, granulated sugar and pepper.

3 Stir well. Garnish with the omelette rounds and coriander leaves.

Chicken and coconut soup

Serves 4-6

Ingredients

- 10oz (315g) skinless, boneless chicken breasts, cut into thin strips
- 4 lemon grass stalks, roots trimmed
- 2 x 13fl oz (400ml) cans coconut milk
- 16fl oz (500ml) chicken stock
- 1in (2½cm) piece fresh galangal, thinly sliced
- 10 black peppercorns, crushed
- 10 kaffir lime leaves
- 3oz (90g) button mushrooms, halved
- 2oz (60g) baby corn cobs, quartered lengthways
- 4tbsp (60ml) fresh lime juice
- 3tbsp (45ml) Thai fish sauce
- Red chilli, scallions (spring onions) and fresh cilantro to garnish.

Method

1 Cut the lower 2in (5cm) from each lemon grass stalk and chop finely. Bruise the remaining pieces of stalk.

2 Bring the coconut milk and chicken stock to boil in a large pan over medium heat. Add the lemon grass, galangal, peppercorns and half the kaffir lime leaves, reduce heat and simmer gently for 10 minutes. Strain the soup into a pan.

3 Return to a low heat, stir in the chicken strips, corn and mushrooms. Simmer for 5-7 minutes until chicken is cooked.

4 Stir in the lime juice, fish sauce and remaining lime leaves. Serve hot garnished with chilli, coriander and spring onions.

Hot and sour prawn soup

Serves 4-6

Ingredients

- 16oz (500g) king prawns
- 32fl oz (1 litre) chicken stock
- 3 lemon grass stalks, roots trimmed
- 10 kaffir lime leaves, torn in half
- 8oz (250g) straw mushrooms, drained
- 3tbsp (45ml) Thai fish sauce
- 4tbsp (60ml) fresh lime juice
- 2tbsp (30ml) chopped spring onions (scallions)
- 1tbsp (15ml) fresh cilantro (coriander) leaves
- 4 fresh red chillies, seeded and thinly sliced
- Salt and ground black pepper as desired

Method

1 Peel the prawns, reserving the shells. Devein the prawns and set aside.

2 Rinse the shells and bring to a boil with the stock.

3 Bruise the lemon grass stalk and add to the stock along with half the lime leaves. Simmer for 5-6 minutes.

4 Strain the stock and reheat. Add the mushrooms and prawns, cook until the prawns turn pink.

5 Stir the fish sauce, lime juice, salt, pepper, spring onion, coriander, chillies and the remaining lime leaves into the soup. Serve hot.

Thai vegetable soup

Serves 4

Ingredients

- 2tbsp (30ml) peanut oil
- 2 cloves garlic
- ½tsp (2½ml) white pepper corns
- Small bunch of cilantro (coriander)
- 16fl oz (500ml) coconut milk
- 3oz (90g) Chinese cabbage
- 1 medium broccoli, coarsely chopped
- 2 medium sized carrots, thinly sliced
- 3oz (90g) button mushrooms, halved
- 20fl oz (600ml) vegetable stock
- 1tsp (5ml) palm sugar
- 3tbsp (45ml) soy sauce
- Cilantro (coriander) for garnish

Method

1 Grind the garlic, white pepper and coriander to a paste. Set aside.

2 Heat oil in a wok or pan, add the paste, sauté until it gives off its aroma. Add the broccoli and carrots. When partially cooked, add the Chinese cabbage and mushrooms. Pour in the vegetable stock and coconut milk, add the palm sugar and soy sauce. Bring to a boil over medium heat.

3 Pour the soup into bowls. Garnish with coriander and serve hot.

Glass noodle salad with shrimp

Serves 4

Ingredients

- 7oz (220g) glass noodles
- 8 baby corn cobs, halved
- 4oz (125g) snow peas
- 1tbsp (15ml) vegetable oil
- 2 garlic cloves, finely chopped
- 1in (2½cm) piece fresh root ginger, finely chopped
- 1 red chilli, seeded and chopped
- 16oz (500g) tiger prawns
- 4 spring onions (scallions) thinly sliced
- 1 lemon grass stalk, thinly shredded

For the dressing

- 1tbsp (15ml) chopped fresh chives
- 1tbsp (15ml) Thai fish sauce
- 1tsp (5ml) soy sauce
- 1tbsp (15ml) peanut oil
- 1tsp (5ml) sesame oil
- 2tbsp (30ml) rice vinegar

Method

1 Put the glass noodles in a bowl and cover with boiling water for 10 minutes until soft. Drain and wash under cold water. Drain again and set aside.

2 Boil the corn cobs and snow peas until tender and crunchy.

3 Mix the ingredients for the dressing.

4 Heat the oil in a large frying pan. Add the garlic, ginger and red chilli and cook for 1 minute. Add tiger prawns and cook until they turn pink. Stir in the spring onions, corn cobs, snow peas and toss lightly to mix.

5 Tip the contents into the bowl containing the glass noodles and toss well. Garnish with lemon grass and serve.

Spicy seafood salad

Serves 4-6

Ingredients

- 8fl oz (250ml) fish stock or water
- 11oz (345g) squid, cleaned and cut into rings
- 12 king prawns
- 12 scallops
- 2oz (60g) glass noodles, soaked in water for 30 minutes
- ½cucumber, cut into batons
- 1 lemon grass stalk, finely chopped
- 2 kaffir lime leaves
- 2 shallots, thinly sliced
- 2 spring onions (scallions) finely chopped
- 2tbsp (30ml) fresh cilantro (coriander) finely chopped
- 5-6 mint leaves, coarsely torn
- 2 red chillies, cut into slivers
- 1tbsp (15ml) lime juice
- 1tbsp (15ml) Thai fish sauce
- Fresh cilantro (coriander) to garnish

Method

1 Bring to boil the fish stock or water in a pan over high heat. Cook each type of the seafood separately in the stock for 3-4 minutes. Remove with a slotted spoon and set aside to cool.

2 Drain the noodles and place them in a serving bowl. Add the cucumber, lemon grass, kaffir lime leaves, shallots, spring onions, coriander, mint and chillies.

3 Pour over the lime juice and fish sauce. Mix well and add the seafood. Toss lightly, garnish with cilantro and serve.

Green chicken curry

Serves 3-4

Ingredients

- 4 skinless, boneless chickens, diced
- 4 spring onions (scallions), trimmed and coarsely chopped
- 2-4 fresh green chillies, seeded and coarsely chopped
- ¾in (2cm) piece fresh root ginger
- 2 garlic cloves
- 1tsp (5ml) Thai fish sauce
- Large bunch of cilantro (coriander)
- Small handful of fresh parsley
- 2-3tbsp (30-45ml) water
- 2tbsp (30ml) oil
- 1 green bell pepper, seeded and thinly sliced
- 32fl oz (1 litre) coconut milk
- Salt and freshly ground pepper as desired

Method

1 Put the spring onions, green chillies, garlic, ginger, fish sauce, coriander and parsley in a blender, add water and grind to a smooth paste.

2 Heat half of the oil in a large frying pan. Cook the diced chicken until brown and transfer to a plate.

3 Heat the remaining oil and stir-fry the green pepper for 3-4 minutes. Add the ground paste, sauté for 2 minutes.

4 On a low flame, bring to boil the chicken and coconut milk. Season with salt and ground pepper. Cover the pan and simmer for 8-10 minutes.

5 When chicken is cooked, add the green pepper and paste. Stir well and cook for 2-3 minutes. Serve hot with rice.

Vegetable Thai curry

Serves 4-6

Ingredients

- 20fl oz (600ml) coconut milk
- 1tbsp (15ml) Thai red curry paste
- 2tsp (10ml) palm sugar
- 4oz (125g) button mushrooms
- 4 baby corn cobs, halved lengthways
- 3oz (90g) green beans, trimmed
- 6oz (185g) firm tofu, rinsed, drained and cut in ¾in (2cm) cubes
- 4 kaffir limes, torn
- 2 fresh red chillies, seeded and sliced
- Fresh cilantro (coriander) to garnish

Method

1 Gently bring to boil one-third of the coconut milk in a wok or pan. Add the red curry paste and palm sugar to the coconut milk.

2 Add the mushrooms, baby corn and green beans. Cook for 3 minutes.

3 Stir in the remaining coconut milk. Add the tofu cubes and simmer for 3-4 minutes.

4 Stir in the kaffir limes and sliced red chillies.

5 Spoon the curry into a serving dish, garnish with cilantro (coriander) leaves and serve hot.

Steamed fish with chilli sauce

Serves 3-4

Ingredients

- 2 medium firm fish such as trout or grouper, scaled and cleaned
- 2tbsp (30ml) rice wine
- 3 fresh red chillies, seeded and thinly sliced
- 4 garlic cloves, finely chopped
- ½in (1cm) piece fresh root ginger, peeled and finely shredded
- 2 lemon grass stalks, crushed and finely chopped
- 2 scallions (spring onions) chopped
- 2tbsp (30ml) Thai fish sauce
- Juice of 1 lime

Method

1 Rinse the fish thoroughly under cold water. Pat dry and slash the skin on both sides.

2 Mix together rice wine, chillies, garlic, shredded ginger, lemon grass and spring onions. Add the fish sauce and lime juice and mix to a paste.

3 Spread the paste evenly on the fish.

4 Put a rack or an upturned plate in the base of the wok. Pour in boiling water to a depth of 2in (5cm). Place the fish on the rack or plate. Cover with a lid and steam for 10-15 minutes until the fish is cooked.

5 Garnish with scallions (spring onions) and ginger. Serve hot.

Beef in peanut sauce

Serves 4-6

Ingredients

- 20fl oz (600ml) coconut milk
- 3tbsp (45ml) Thai red curry paste
- 3tbsp (45ml) Thai fish sauce
- 2tbsp (30ml) palm sugar
- 2 lemon grass stalks, crushed
- 16oz (500g) rump (round) steak, cut into thin strips
- 3oz (90g) roasted peanuts, ground
- 2 fresh red chillies
- 5 kaffir lime leaves, torn
- Salt and ground pepper as desired

Method

1 Pour half of the coconut milk into a large and heavy pan. Place over low heat and bring to boil stirring constantly.

2 Stir in the red curry paste and cook for 2-3 minutes until the mixture is thoroughly blended.

3 Add the fish sauce, palm sugar and crushed lemon grass stalks. Mix well until color deepens.

4 Add the beef and peanuts. Gradually add the remaining coconut milk and bring to a boil.

5 Stir constantly for 8-10 minutes until the beef is cooked. Add the chillies and lime leaves. Season to taste with salt & pepper and serve hot.

Stir-Fried vegetables with sesame and rice

Serves 4 as an accompaniment

Ingredients

- 1tbsp (15ml) peanut oil
- 2 cloves garlic, crushed
- 3 green chillies, chopped finely
- I medium white onion chopped coarsely
- 1 large carrot sliced thinly
- 1 large red capsicum sliced thinly
- 4oz (125g) green beans, trimmed
- 9oz (280g) broccoli, chopped coarsely
- 14oz (440g) baby corn, halved lengthways
- 2tbsp (30ml) soy sauce
- 2tbsp (30ml) sesame seeds, toasted
- 1tsp (5ml) corn flour, mixed in 3tbsp (45ml) water
- 1tsp (5ml) mild sweet chilli sauce

Method

1 Heat oil in a wok, stir-fry garlic, green chillies, onion and carrot until soft.

2 Add capsicum, beans and broccoli; stir-fry.

3 Add corn, blended cornflour, soy sauce and sweet chilli sauce. Stir-fry until the sauce thickens.

4 Garnish with sesame seeds and serve hot with rice.

Beef fried rice

Serves 4

Ingredients

- 16fl oz (500ml) coconut milk
- 11oz (345g) jasmine rice, rinsed
- 2tbsp (30ml) peanut oil
- 4 garlic cloves
- 2 small onions, finely chopped
- 2in (5cm) piece of fresh root ginger, grated
- 8oz (250g) beef steak, cut into ½in (1cm) dice
- 1 red bell pepper, seeded and sliced
- 1tsp (5ml) chilli oil
- 2tsp (10ml) hot curry powder
- 2 eggs, beaten
- Salt to taste
- 1 tomato and cucumber sliced thinly for garnish

Method

1 Pour the coconut milk into a pan and add the rice. Bring to a boil, reduce heat and cook for 12 minutes, or until the rice is tender. Set aside to cool.

2 Heat the oil in a wok, add the garlic, onion and ginger and stir fry over medium heat for 2 minutes.

3 Push the onion mixture to the sides of the wok, add the beef to the centre and stir-fry for 2 minutes. Add the rice and toss well. Stir-fry over a high heat for about 3 minutes more until the beef is cooked well.

4 Stir in the sliced red pepper, chilli oil, curry powder and salt to taste. Toss over the heat for 1 minute.

5 Stir in the beaten eggs and cook for another minute. Garnish and decorate the plate with tomato and cucumber. Serve hot.

Spicy fried noodles with meat

Serves 4-6

Ingredients

- 8oz (250g) egg thread noodles
- 4tbsp (60ml) vegetable oil
- 4 garlic cloves, finely chopped
- 6oz (185g) pork fillet (tenderloin), sliced into thin strips
- 5oz (155g) skinless, boneless chicken breast, sliced into thin strips
- 4oz (125g) prawns, peeled
- 3tbsp (45ml) fresh lemon juice
- 3tbsp (45ml) Thai fish sauce
- 2tbsp (30ml) brown sugar
- 2 eggs, beaten
- 1 red chilli, seeded and finely chopped
- 2oz (60g) bean sprouts
- 4tbsp (60ml) roasted peanuts, chopped
- 3 spring onions (scallions) cut into 2in (5cm) lengths
- 3tbsp (45ml) chopped fresh cilantro (coriander) leaves

Method

1 Bring a large pan of water to boil. Add the noodles, remove the pan from the heat and leave for 5 minutes.

2 Heat 3tbsp (45ml) of oil in a wok, add the garlic, pork and chicken and stir-fry until lightly brown. Add the prawns and stir-fry for another 3-4 minutes.

3 Drain the noodles and add to the wok with the remaining oil. Add the lemon juice, fish sauce & brown sugar. Toss all the ingredients together.

4 Pour the beaten eggs over the noodles and stir-fry until almost set, and add the chilli and bean sprouts.

5 Place the noodles in a serving bowl and mix in the spring onions, coriander and roasted peanuts. Serve hot.

Thai fried noodles with tofu and shrimps

Serves 4-6

Ingredients

- 16 raw prawns
- 12oz (375g) rice noodles
- 3tbsp (45ml) vegetable oil
- 1tbsp (15ml) chopped garlic
- 2 eggs, lightly beaten
- 3oz (90g) fried tofu, cut into small cubes
- ½tsp (2½ml) dried chilli flakes
- 1 large bunch garlic chives cut into 2in (5cm) lengths
- 8oz (155g) bean sprouts
- 2oz (60g) roasted peanuts, coarsely ground
- 1tsp (5ml) granulated sugar
- 1tbsp (15ml) dark soy sauce
- 2tbsp (30ml) Thai fish sauce
- 2tbsp (30ml) tamarind juice
- Fresh cilantro (coriander) leaves to garnish

Method

1 Peel the prawns with the tails intact and devein.

2 Place the rice noodles in a bowl and pour enough warm water to cover it. Soak for 20-30 minutes, drain and set aside.

3 Heat 1tbsp (15ml) of the oil in a wok.

4 Stir-fry garlic until golden. Stir in the prawns and cook for 1-2 minutes, until pink. Remove and set aside.

5 Heat the remaining oil, add the tofu cubes and dried chilli flakes. Add the noodles and stir-fry for about 5 minutes.

6 Add the garlic chives, half the bean sprouts and peanuts. Add the granulated sugar, soy sauce, fish sauce and tamarind juice. Mix well and cook until the noodles are heated through.

7 Pour egg mixture into the wok, cook for 1 minute, add the prawns and mix with the noodles. Serve topped with the remaining bean sprouts and peanuts. Garnish with cilantro (coriander) leaves and serve hot.

Sweet and hot noodles with vegetables and chicken

Serves 4-6

Ingredients

- 4oz (125g) dried rice noodles
- 5oz (155g) skinless, boneless chicken breast, sliced into thin strips
- 1in (2½cm) piece fresh root ginger, sliced into thin batons
- 3 garlic cloves, crushed
- 2tbsp (30ml) peanut oil
- 4oz (125g) drained canned bamboo shoots, sliced into batons
- 2 medium carrots
- 3oz (90g) bean sprouts
- 1 small white cabbage, shredded
- 2tbsp (30ml) Thai fish sauce
- 2tbsp (30ml) soy sauce
- 2tbsp (30ml) plum sauce
- 2tsp (10ml) sesame oil
- 1tbsp (15ml) palm sugar
- Juice of 1 lime
- Small bunch of fresh cilantro (coriander) leaves

Method

1 Cook the noodles, drain and set aside.

2 Heat the peanut oil in a wok, stir-fry ginger and garlic. Add the chicken and stir-fry until golden brown.

3 Add the bamboo shoots and stir-fry for 3-4 minutes. Add the carrots, bean sprouts and cabbage for a further 3 minutes.

4 Stir in the sauces, sesame oil, sugar and lime juice. Add in the cilantro (coriander) leaves, toss to mix and serve hot.

Chicken curry with Thai basil, peppers and rice

Serves 4

Ingredients

For the green curry paste

- 2 green chillies
- 1tbsp (15ml) coriander leaves
- 2g lemon grass
- ¼oz (10g) fresh ginger root
- 1 fresh kaffir lime leaf
- 2oz (60g) spring onions
- 2 cloves garlic
- ½tsp (2½ml) coriander seeds, crushed
- ½tsp (2½ml) cumin seeds, crushed

For the curry

- 1 poulard, about 48oz (1500g), jointed
- 3tbsp (45ml) peanut oil
- 6fl oz (200ml) chicken stock
- Salt & freshly ground pepper as desired
- 16fl oz (500ml) coconut milk
- 6½oz (200g) mixed peppers (red, yellow, green)
- 3oz (90g) mangetout
- Juice of ½ lime
- Thai basil leaves

Method

For the curry paste

1 Halve the chillies, remove the stalks, seeds and membranes and finely chop the flesh. Finely chop the coriander leaves, finely dice the lemon grass and peel and dice the ginger. Shred the kaffir lime leaf. Trim the spring onions, peel the garlic and finely chop both. Put all these ingredients into a liquidizer with the coriander and cumin seeds and blend to a fine paste.

2 Skin and bone the poulard and cut the meat into approximately 1¼in (3cm) pieces.

3 Heat the oil in a wok or a large frying pan and fry the meat for 2-3 minutes, a few pieces at a time, turning frequently, until firm and golden brown. Return all the meat to the wok, add the curry paste and stir-fry for 1 minute.

4 Add the chicken stock, bring to a boil and season with salt and pepper (if necessary). Add half of the coconut milk, cover with a lid on and cook gently for 5 minutes.

5 Halve the peppers, remove the stalks, seeds and membranes and cut the flesh into ½in (1cm) diamonds. Cut the ends off the mangetout and cut the pods in half crosswise.

6 Add the rest of the coconut milk and the vegetables and cook without the lid for a further 8-12 minutes. Add the lime juice and check the seasoning. Serve garnished with basil leaves.

Banana fritters

Serves 4

Ingredients

- 4oz (125g) plain (all purpose) flour
- ½tsp (2½ml) bicarbonate of soda
- A pinch of salt
- 2tbsp (30ml) granulated sugar
- 1 egg, beaten
- 6tbsp (90ml) water
- 1tbsp (15ml) sesame seeds
- 4 firm bananas
- Vegetable oil for deep frying

Method

1 Sift the flour, bicarbonate of soda and salt into a large bowl. Stir in the granulated sugar and the egg, and whisk in enough water to make a thin batter.

2 Whisk in the sesame seeds.

3 Peel the bananas. Carefully cut each one in half lengthways, then in half crossways to make 16 pieces of about the same size.

4 Heat the oil in a wok. Dip the banana pieces in the batter and fry until golden brown. Drain on a kitchen towel and serve hot with honey or vanilla ice cream.

Sticky rice with mango wedges

Serves 4

Ingredients

- 4oz (125g) sticky (glutinous) white rice
- 6fl oz (190ml) thick coconut milk
- 3tbsp (45ml) granulated sugar
- A pinch of salt
- 2 ripe mangoes
- ½tsp (2½ml) toasted peanuts for garnish

Method

1 Rinse the glutinous rice thoroughly and leave to soak overnight in a bowl of fresh, cold water.

2 Drain and spread the rice in an even layer in a steamer lined with cheese cloth. Cover and steam for about 20 minutes or until the rice is tender.

3 Reserve 3tbsp (45ml) of the top of the coconut milk and combine the rest with the sugar and salt in a saucepan. Bring to a boil, stirring until the sugar dissolves, then pour into a bowl and leave it to cool.

4 Transfer the rice to a bowl and pour over the cooled coconut milk mixture. Stir well and leave to stand for 10-15 minutes.

5 Peel the mangoes and cut the flesh into slices. Place around the plate and drizzle over the remaining coconut milk. Garnish with toasted peanuts.

Conversion guide

The Conversion guide given below is not an exact equivalent but an approximation, to make your measuring easier.

Dry Measures

Imperial	Metric
½oz	15g
1oz	30g
2oz	60g
3oz	90g
4oz (¼lb)	125g
5oz	155g
6oz	185g
7oz	220g
8oz (½lb)	250g
9oz	280g
10oz	315g
11oz	345g
12oz (¾lb)	375g
13oz	410g
14oz	440g
15oz	470g
16oz (1 lb)	500g
24oz (1½lb)	750g
32oz (2lb)	1Kg

Liquid Measures

Imperial	Metric
1fluid oz	30ml
2fluid oz	60ml
3fluid oz	100ml
4fluid oz	125ml
5fluid oz (¼pint /1gill)	150ml
6fluid oz	190ml
8fluid oz	250ml
10fluid oz (½pint)	300ml
16fluid oz	500ml
20fluid oz (1pint)	600ml
1¾pints	1000ml (1 litre)

Conversion guide

Cup & Spoon Measures

Imperial	Metric
¼tsp	1ml
½tsp	2½ml
1tsp	5ml
1tbsp	15ml
¼cup	60ml
½cup	125ml
1cup	250ml

Helpful Measures

Imperial	Metric
⅛in	3mm
¼in	6mm
½in	1cm
¾in	2cm
1in	2.5cm
2in	5cm
2½in	6cm
3in	8cm
4in	10cm
5in	13cm
6in	15cm
7in	18cm
8in	20cm
9in	23cm
10in	25cm
11in	28cm
12in	30cm

Oven temperatures

	°F (Fahrenheit)	°C (Celsius)	Gas Mark
Very low	250	120	1
Low	300	150	2
Moderately low	325	160	3
Moderate	350-375	180-190	4
Moderately hot	400-425	200-210	5
Hot	450-475	220-230	6
Very hot	500-525	240-250	7

Glossary

Basil Thai holy basil lends a distinctive flavor to many Thai dishes.

Chillies, green & red Green and red chillies are a central ingredient in Thai cuisine.

Coconut milk is used as a sauce and thickener, or simply added in order to give a coconut flavor to soups, curries, noodles, vegetables, fish and meat dishes, as well as desserts. For good quality and flavor, look for 'thick' as opposed to 'thin' coconut milk.

Cilantro also called coriander or Chinese parsley is another herb commonly found in Thai cuisine.

Fish Sauce is a salty liquid made from small fish. It is used widely in Thai cooking, and can be added to any Thai dish in place of salt.

Galangal is a type of ginger used commonly in the Thai kitchen. Also referred to as Siamese Ginger, it has a slightly milder taste than the North American variety, and can be distinguished by its reddish skin.

Garlic in Thai cooking is always used in its fresh state, usually minced along with other ingredients in a paste.

Kaffir Lime Leaves Kaffir Lime is a dark green fruit distinctly different from the limes commonly used, and easily distinguished by its knobby skin. In Thai cuisine, it is mainly the leaves that are used, adding a unique lime flavor to soups, curries, and sauces.

Lemon grass provides a fragrant and distinct lemon flavor to many Thai dishes. Chefs use the lower, bulbous part of the lemon grass, stalk, usually pounding or crushing it first before adding it to the dish.

Lime is used more often than lemon in Thai cooking.

Mushrooms such as shiitake, straw, and wood ear are common ingredients in Thai soups, noodles, and stir-fries.

Noodles The typical rice noodle in Thailand, commonly referred to as "Rick Stick", is long, thin, and flat. But Thai chefs also use rice vermicelli noodles, thin egg and wheat noodles, as well as a type of noodle known as "cellophane" also called "bean thread" or "glass" noodles. These are extremely thin and become clear when you cook them. The noodles are especially healthy, as they are made from mung beans instead of rice or wheat.

Oil is required for nearly all Thai dishes. Thai cooks commonly use coconut or palm oil which have a low-smoke rate and do not break down quickly. Other good alternatives include sunflower, corn, peanut, and other nut oils.

Red curry paste

Ingredients

- 3 shallots, sliced
- 1 stalk lemon grass
- 1-3 red chillies (depending on desired spiciness) or 1-3 tsp (5-15ml) Thai red chilli sauce
- 3 cloves garlic
- 1 thumb-size piece galangal, peeled and sliced (may be substituted with ginger)
- ¼tsp (1ml) white pepper (may be substituted with black pepper)
- 1tsp (5ml) ground cumin
- 2tbsp (30ml) coriander seeds, ground with mortar & pestle (or a coffee grinder)
- 3tbsp (45ml) fish sauce or soy sauce
- 1 kaffir lime leaf
- 1tsp (5ml) shrimp paste (optional)
- 1tsp (5ml) sugar
- 1½tbsp (22ml)regular chilli powder
- 2¾fl oz (80ml) coconut milk

Preparation

Place all ingredients in a food processor or blender and process well.

Rice Thai Rice is often called "scented" or "jasmine" due to its fragrant aroma. Another variety of Thai rice is sweet rice, also called "sticky" for its texture. Sweet rice is used in many Thai desserts including cakes and puddings.

Shallots are commonly used in Thailand and come in all sizes and colors, including purple. If shallots aren't available at your local grocery store or are too expensive, a good substitute would be a combination of white cooking onion and garlic.

Soy Sauce, light and dark are a mainstay in all Asian cuisines, including Thai. "Light" refers to regular soy sauce, while "dark" is literally darker and stronger in flavor. Vegetarians should note that light soy sauce can be substituted for fish sauce in most recipes. Thai chefs also use sweet soy sauce in certain dishes. Also known as tamari.

Tamarind is a kind of sweet and sour fruit that grows in a pod. In Thai cooking it is used mostly in savory dishes. It is more convenient to purchase tamarind puree and it tastes just as good.

Tofu is used in a variety of forms in Thai cooking, from fresh to deep fried, from soft to extra firm. Tofu can be used as a meat substitute in many Thai dishes.

Turmeric powders are widely available in spice sections of grocery stores and may offer the same health benefits as fresh. Turmeric is used frequently in Thai curries and other savory dishes.